When Life
STINKS

how to deal with your bad moods, blues, and depression

Other books in the sunscreen series:

feeling freakish?
how to be comfortable in your own skin

just us girls
secrets to feeling good about yourself, inside and out

my parents are getting divorced
how to keep it together when your mom and dad are splitting up

sex explained
honest answers to your questions about guys & girls, your changing body, and what really happens during sex

drugs explained
the real deal on alcohol, pot, ecstasy, and more

When Life
STINKS

305.235
Piquemal

how to deal with your bad moods, blues, and depression

Michel Piquemal with Melissa Daly
illustrated by Olivier Tossan

Buhler High School
Library Media Center
Unified School District #313

sunscreen

Production Manager: Jonathan Lopes

Library of Congress Cataloging-in-Publication Data

Piquemal, Michel, 1954–
[Ado blues. English]
When life stinks : how to deal with your bad moods, blues, and depression / Michel Piquemal with Melissa Daly ; illustrated by Olivier Tossan ; [translated by Jane Moseley].
p. cm.
Includes bibliographical references and index.
ISBN 0-8109-4932-6
1. Teenagers. 2. Adolescent psychology. 3. Teenagers—Health and hygiene. 4. Depression in adolescence. I. Daly, Melissa. II. Tossan, Olivier. III. Title.
HQ796.P5213 2004
305.235—dc22
2004013001

Text copyright © 2004 Michel Piquemal with Melissa Daly
Illustrations © 1996, 2004 Oliver Tossan
Book series design by Higashi Glaser Design

Translated by Jane Moseley

Published in 2004 by Amulet Books an imprint of Harry N. Abrams, Incorporated. 100 Fifth Avenue, New York, NY 10011
www.abramsbooks.com

All rights reserved. No part of the contents of this book may be reproduced without the written permission of the publisher.
Printed and bound in China
1 3 5 7 9 10 8 6 4 2

Abrams is a subsidiary of

LA MARTINIÈRE
GROUPE

For Cécile

contents

9	introduction

phase 1: FAREWELL TO CHILDHOOD

12	what's wrong with me?
14	old school/new school
16	freaky friday
17	love is in the air
18	let's talk about sex
20	a whole new world
22	don't panic
23	you're not alone
24	time to take off the training wheels

phase 4: PARENTS AND TEACHERS

66	anger and aggression
67	give me some space!
68	parents just don't understand
69	how the adult mind works
71	overprotective parents
73	slamming doors
74	keeping your distance
75	a time of paradox
76	emerging opinions
78	necessary roughness
80	cut the cord
81	brick walls
82	ghost parents
84	institutionalized
86	authority or authoritarians?
87	labels
88	don't give up

phase 2: ADOLESCENT BLUES

- 28 the metamorphosis
- 29 sex: the big questions
- 31 boys and body talk
- 32 talk about it
- 33 hello, anxiety!
- 34 but who am I?
- 35 am I ugly?
- 36 the first steps
- 38 mood swings
- 39 let yourself go
- 40 if only I were more like . . .
- 41 mom and dad's clone
- 43 we always hurt the ones we love

phase 3: BANISH THE BLUES!

- 46 help!
- 47 talk to someone
- 48 a real friend
- 49 look in the mirror
- 50 how do you make new friends?
- 52 something in common
- 53 get moving!
- 54 so much to choose from
- 56 your safety valve
- 58 set yourself free
- 59 create something
- 61 poetic license

phase 5: TOO MUCH, IT'S TOO MUCH

- 92 a terrible time
- 94 stumbling blocks
- 95 a mountain too high
- 96 what to do?
- 97 find a way out
- 98 when it's not just in your head
- 100 running away and suicide
- 102 open arms
- 103 the sun'll come out . . .
- 105 useful information
- 106 bibliography
- 107 index

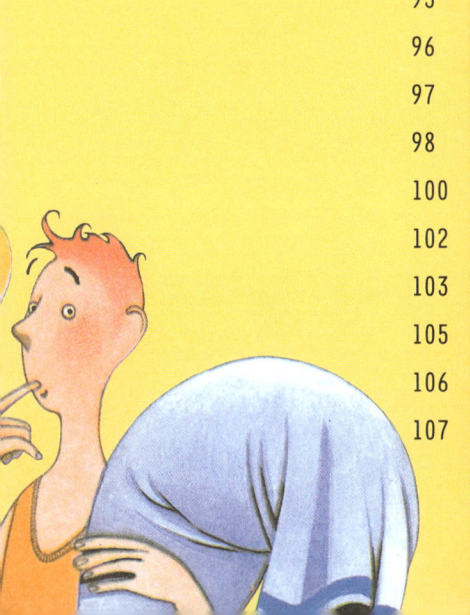

WHY DO I FEEL SO BAD ABOUT MYSELF AND EVERYONE ELSE? WILL I EVER BE HAPPY AGAIN? CAN ANYTHING MAKE ME FEEL BETTER? WHY DO LITTLE THINGS BOTHER ME SO MUCH? WHY DOES LIFE STINK?

introduction

So you're not a kid anymore; you're finally old enough for life to really start getting good. This is when it's all supposed to happen: boyfriends and girlfriends, varsity sports, being treated more like a grown-up. But now that you're here, it's not actually living up to the hype. Nothing's going like you thought it would, and all you feel is down. Sound familiar? This is the way it happens for a lot of kids. Right about now, everything is changing—your school, your body, your friends—and it's a lot to deal with. This sticky time between childhood and adulthood is often as frustrating and confusing as it is exciting.

It's kind of like stepping up onto the high diving board and then realizing you're not really sure you want to jump in. What if you belly flop? What if it hurts? What if everyone laughs? Feelings of sadness, hopelessness, or anxiety can pop up now and then, or they can set up camp in your psyche and refuse to leave. When these feelings interfere with your sleeping and eating habits, when your favorite things no longer make you happy, and when all this lasts for more than two weeks straight, it's called depression. But your situation is likely not that serious; what you're feeling is probably a case of the teenage blues—and it's extremely common. This book will help you sort things out, understand what's going on in your head, and banish those bad feelings for good.

phase 1

KEEP IT IN PERSPECTIVE

farewell

love is in the air

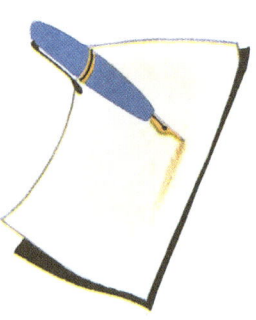

everything's different

a brand-new body

to

DON'T PANIC!

CHILDHOOD

passionate moments

what's wrong

You might be ten or fifteen or in between. You might be a boy or a girl, living in the city or suburbs or country, with both parents or one parent or your grandparents. But no matter who you are or where you live, you are likely experiencing the feelings and symptoms of adolescence. There are physical changes and emotional ones. Some are kind of cool, and others are really awful and annoying. While "adolescence" is an idea that people came up with in the first half of the twentieth century, puberty, on the other hand, is a biological fact, an inescapable part of life. Based on some of the facts you hear about it, it sounds a little like some infectious disease: "In females, premenstrual syndrome may cause muscle aches, bloating, mood swings, and increased appetite. In males, onset of ejaculation has been linked to spontaneous erections and nocturnal emissions. Persons affected by puberty can be identified by red, pus-filled spots on the face and an ever-increasing amount of hair."

OK, so puberty isn't really a disease. In fact, most of the physical changes probably won't even bother you too much. They're just part of growing up. But they do mark a period of transition and, as often happens during times of change, life can get more difficult for a while. You may no longer feel like the happy kid you were just last year. The blues and depression can hit hard during puberty. We won't try and tell you not to worry, that whatever you're anxious about now will seem like no big deal down the road. But we will say that you're going to get through it. And we're here to help you do that.

with me?

old school/new

One of the biggest and most obvious changes of adolescence is heading off to junior high or middle school.

Let's rewind for a second. A little while back, you were happy and comfortable in your elementary school, being taught by the same teacher *all* day long. You were in the highest grade and you and your friends whom you'd known since kindergarten ruled the school. Now, suddenly, you've been catapulted into a huge anonymous building, maybe even with a whole new crop of unfamiliar faces.

You have to remember the names of a dozen teachers instead of just one, and there are a million classrooms to find. "Where is third-period biology?" "Room 242, no, 327, fourth floor, Building B." "Is it geography with Mr. Brown today?" "No, this week it's science with Mrs. Simpson." And God forbid you bring your geography textbook instead of your science one—detention! It probably feels like this kind of thing happens to you every day.

school

You have to be much more independent now, which has both advantages and disadvantages. You're in charge of what you do in between classes and maybe after school, too, and that can take some getting used to. Before, decisions were almost always made for you. Now, you have to make your mind up on your own. The other kids in your class are in the same boat, and going along with the decisions they make won't always steer you down the right path. There'll be kids who pick fights, kids who steal, kids who do drugs. It's up to you whether you want to follow in their footsteps or blaze your own trail.

freaky friday

Luckily, most of the physical changes you're experiencing will happen more gradually than your start at a new school. You won't just wake up one day in the body of Jamie Lee Curtis and be forced to wear your mom's suit and heels. Although at some point you might just wake up, look in the mirror, and think, when did I start to look like such an adult?

In a kid's body, you felt comfortable tearing off your clothes at pool parties and jumping right in. You let your dad pick you up on his shoulders and throw you around. Now, the very same body that used to fit so well into your mom and dad's arms and was just the right size for goodnight hugs has undergone a complete transformation. Your jeans are too tight and it seems like you have to buy new shoes every three months. (On the other hand, your suddenly giant hands can now grip a basketball like never before!) Still, sometimes you feel like you're carrying around someone else's big, awkward body.

The disturbing part comes when you start to feel a little silly about hugging your mom, since you're a foot taller than her now. Or it starts to seem weird to sit on your dad's lap now that you almost look too old to be his daughter. Not to mention that you've got all these thoughts and questions going around in your head about guys and girls and sex and stuff that you would die if your parents knew about.

love is in
the air

Suddenly all anyone's talking about is boyfriends and girlfriends and hooking up. Somehow it creeps into every situation and relationship, altering the delicate balance of things. A guy and a girl can't talk in the hallway without it being a big deal, a possible romance. A couple of years ago, boys were boys through and through, reading comic books, playing football in the backyard, spending hours mastering the Xbox. Girls—well, girls might have already started getting crushes, but there wasn't ever really the possibility that something might actually happen between a guy and a girl. Now, whether or not you "get noticed" by the opposite sex can make or break your year.

let's talk about
sex

Once the first few couples have had their first kisses, everyone starts talking about sex. But at this point, that's really all it is—talk. Guys might get their hands on a dirty magazine now and then or tell a few hundred X-rated jokes. Girls, unfortunately, might discuss whether this friend or that is going too far too quickly with too many guys. But for the most part, they all have one thing in common: they don't really know what they're talking about. Sex is a big deal, and whether you even realize it, the idea of it can cause some serious anxiety. Everybody's anxious about coming off like they know too little—or too much. Everybody's curious about what happens when a guy and girl get together—but they're also a little nervous about finding out. Everybody worries about whether they're attractive to the opposite sex. And then, ultimately, there's the question about how to tell when you're in love and when you're ready for sex.

It helps to have role models, happy couples you know, like your mom and dad or your aunt and uncle. Although not all the couples you look at will be perfect. What about famous couples or couples in movies? They seem pretty perfect, right? The problem there is that they're not actually real. (Even the real-life celebrity couples aren't "real" in the sense that you don't see the whole picture—you only see what they show on TV and in magazines.) So along with making you feel like you'll never look as good as they do (by the way—all those pictures in magazines are totally airbrushed!), movie stars aren't the greatest people to model your behavior after.

You also shouldn't feel like whatever your friends are doing in their relationships is automatically what you should do, too. While it's great to have role models, when it comes down to it, only you know what's right for you.

a whole new world

Some of the stuff you're going through is just a part of growing up. But if you're like a lot of kids—especially bright, well-informed ones—it's also what's going on in the world right now that's getting you down. Just about the time you're starting to think about getting an after-school job, maybe one of your parents gets laid off at work due to corporate downsizing. And now that you've fallen in love with the new kid in your class and can't think about anything but making out, your health teacher begins explaining all the different sexually transmitted diseases out there—including deadly ones, like AIDS.

Sure, it's good to be aware of the dangers that lurk around certain street corners, but why does the news only report that six people died in

a train wreck over the weekend and never that thirty million people traveled safely, without any trouble? Why do they have to tell you that one child drowned instead of how hundreds of thousands of others had a wonderful time playing Marco Polo and splashing around like demented ducklings? Sometimes knowing all the risks in life only makes you feel worse. It's like boarding a plane and having the flight attendant inform you of exactly how many crashes there have been in the past ten years, complete with a list of all the victims. You'll want to walk across the country instead!

Some kids carry the weight of the world on their shoulders. Thinking about the homeless, the hurt, and even the persecuted people in far-away countries keeps them up at night. It might seem like your parents didn't have to deal with the kind of crazy stuff you do—and to some extent, that's true—every generation has had its unique challenges. The good news is that every generation pulled through. And so will yours.

don't panic

The point of the last few chapters is not to remind you of all the stuff you have to worry about. The real goal is to reassure you that you're not unusual and you're not alone. In fact, most of the kids in your class are probably having all the same feelings. Even the obnoxious guy who acts like he's the hottest thing in school—he's probably completely insecure. He brags and puts other people down to make himself feel better. Even your parents and teachers have been through similar experiences. If you ask them at the right time, your dad might just tell you about how nervous he was before he kissed a girl for the first time. Your math teacher might admit that she was teased about her glasses all through middle school. Hearing about the trials and tribulations of their youth—and seeing that they eventually outgrew all the anxiety and the drama that you're dealing with right now—can make you feel a lot less isolated.

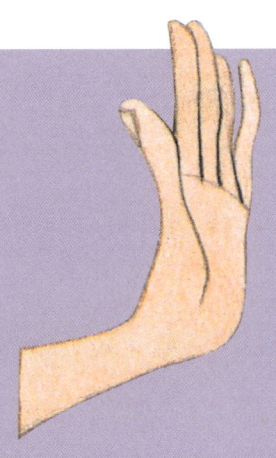

you're not alone

The physical changes associated with adolescence have existed since the first teenager. What's different today in America is the lack of the "rites of passage" that exist in other cultures. Rites of passage are rituals or events that a young person goes through in order to pass on to the next stage of life. After completing the ritual, the child is considered an adult—an immediate and smooth transition. For example, historically, young boys of the Native American Lakota tribe traditionally reached manhood as soon as they took part in a war expedition. Today, in the Casamance villages of Senegal, boys assume the status of adults after undergoing the ritual of circumcision. The boys spend several days in a sacred part of the bush with their elders and on their return they are treated as men by the entire village. In these societies, the passage into adulthood is not an individual experience but a collective one, in which everyone in the community participates.

In the nineteenth century, it was common for children of farmers and laborers to start working at the age of eleven or twelve, which sort of made them into adults, in a way. Today, young people go to school until they're at least sixteen—most often till they're eighteen, and for college-bound students, until they're twenty-two. This makes the adolescent period longer in our society, which is a good thing because you get more prep time before you're thrown into grown-up responsibilities. But it also puts you in a weird in-between mode, where you're not really a child anymore, but you're also not an adult yet, either. You're caught between two worlds.

time to take off the training
wheels

So would we be better off if we still had traditional rites of passage like other cultures? That's open to debate (after all, some of them sound pretty harsh!). What's clearer is that not having them has created this uncertain in-between period called adolescence, which certainly doesn't make life much easier. The advantage of traditional rituals was that afterward, everybody knew you were grown-up. There was no questioning it. Nowadays, young people seem to have to prove themselves constantly.

This probably factors into why some kids are tempted by cigarettes, alcohol, and drugs. They think (incorrectly, by the way) that smoking or getting high will give them adult status, an air of independence in the eyes of the other kids and maybe even their parents. They could be using these substances to replace the missing rites of passage. Unfortunately, these substances can be deadly. And risking your life just to get to the next stage of it faster doesn't make sense.

So basically, to summarize, this time in your life could be a pretty bumpy ride. But it's also a pretty amazing, hard-to-beat one. The things you discover, experience, and feel passionate about will never seem quite so intense again. Your first kiss, first driving lesson, first trip abroad . . . You have your whole life ahead of you.

Every day could be the day when something exciting and new happens. Now that everything you've been waiting for is almost within reach, you probably feel like speeding through it to get to the really good stuff. You finally get to hang out on your own—no parents—and it's the perfect opportunity for you to explore the big wide world of new possibilities out there. The training wheels are coming off! It's frightening, we know, but at the same time, it's kind of a rush, don't you think?

Sometimes you'll want to just get this part of your life over and done with, but it plays a vital, irreplaceable role in the way your personality develops. It can be one of the best times ever if you grab life with both hands rather than wait nervously for it to happen to you. Don't sit this one out—be brave and courageous, and the incredible person you become will thank you for it.

phase 2

am I normal?

ADOLESCENT

hello, anxiety!

IF THE RIDE GETS TOO BUMPY

BLUES

SEX: THE BIG QUESTIONS

i'm so ugly!

WHO CAN I CONFIDE IN?

the
metamorphosis

Not feeling comfortable in your own skin lately? That's to be expected. (Zits don't make it any easier, do they?) You've most likely had enough health classes at school to know what's going on with your body. Still, it's normal to be a little obsessed with it right now. Since it's sort of a weird thing to discuss with your friends, you're left wondering:

Am I developing too quickly? Not quickly enough? Am I behind everyone else? Am I ahead of them? Don't think you're the only person who's counting underarm hairs or checking out your chest at every possible angle in the mirror.

All these changes indicate that you're developing sexually. Once a girl has her period and a guy ejaculates, they're then physically capable of making babies. But obviously, in our society, you're supposed to wait till you're a lot older for that. So that leaves you here, stuck with this big adult body while everyone's still treating you like a little kid. No wonder you're feeling a bit confused.

sex: the big
questions

So, for boys, you're looking at big-time hair growth on your legs, face, chest, underarms, and pubic area; your penis will grow, your voice will get lower, and you will ejaculate for the first time. Girls, you'll grow underarm and pubic hair, grow breasts and wider hips, and get your first period. And all of this is ripe material for bad jokes by obnoxious kids trying to deflect attention away from their own body insecurities. But as much as people joke about sex, and as much as you hear about sexual liberation and all that, it still remains a taboo subject.

Lots of parents secretly hope that their kids will stay all "sugar and spice" forever and that they won't ever have to deal with sensitive issues like sex. Everyone—parents included—dreads that embarrassing talk about "the birds and the bees," when Mom or Dad sits you down to talk about two people loving each other "in a special way" and tries to explain where babies come from. Some parents would like to believe that their children know everything already, having seen it all on TV or the Internet—so they can get out of having "the talk." But watching explicit sex scenes in movies just doesn't cut it. You need to get the whole picture, and you need to be able to ask questions.

Often daughters are more likely to have talked to their moms about this stuff, since the eventual need for maxi pads and tampons sort of makes it necessary at a certain point. So where does that leave the boys?

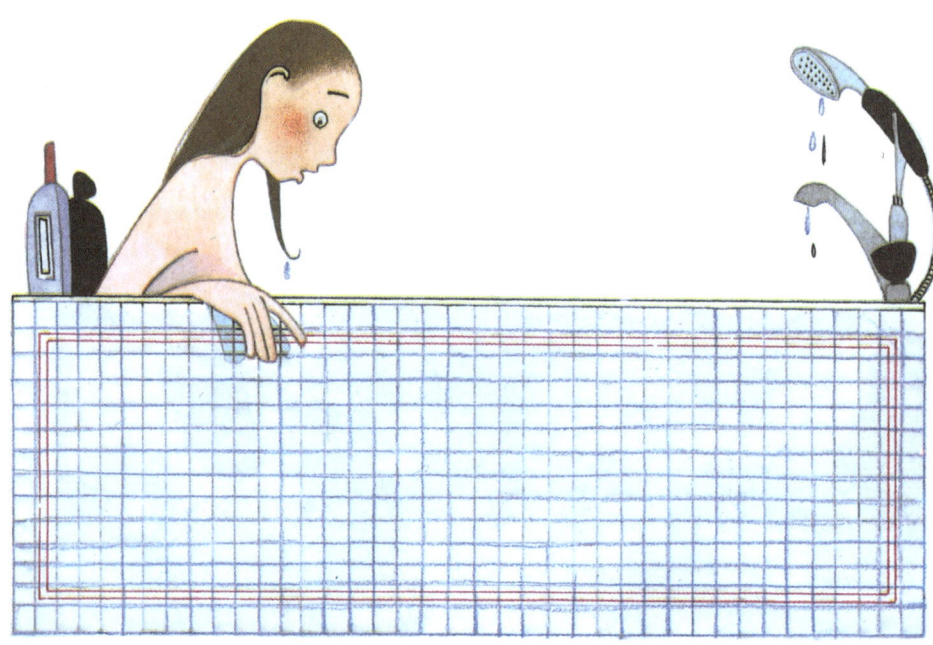

boys and
body talk

It's not often that you find a dad who has talked to his son about "wet dreams"—the expression used to describe something that happens to all adolescent boys at about the age of thirteen. One morning you wake up and discover the sheet is wet with a whitish, sticky substance—don't worry, it's just sperm. It means you had an erection during your sleep and ejaculated. Of course you don't want your mom to see it—but of course she's the one who makes the beds!

Seriously, though, it's nothing to be embarrassed about. It's sort of, well, a rite of passage—you have now become fertile. You've reached physical maturity, and you can now have children.

talk about it

Don't feel like you need to go to extreme lengths to try to hide what happened. (Is anything worth having to do laundry to cover?) It's happened to all the men you know—your father, your uncle, your older

brother. You don't need to announce it at the breakfast table, but if the topic somehow comes up in conversation among the guys of the family and someone asks, feel free to answer truthfully. It couldn't hurt to have someone to talk to about it. Same goes for your friends. Some of them have probably had a wet dream but may be keeping it to themselves because they think it's something to be ashamed of.

The same advice applies to girls as well. As much as you've learned in school and from your friends, you're bound to have more questions—little things you never thought of before but which you now need to know. Like is it OK to flush tampon applicators? (It depends on the type of tampon and the type of plumbing you have.) Or, can you go swimming while using a maxi pad? (You can, but a tampon might be the best, most discreet option.) Your mom can help you with all this stuff—you just have to ask.

hello, anxiety!

So we've covered the physical side of things. But what's often more troubling to teenagers are the changes inside. There's a good chance you've been fighting with your family a little more frequently these days. You might also be having problems with friends—maybe you're losing touch with some of the people you used to hang out with and starting to gravitate toward others. Friendship shake-ups are extremely common around this age.

That's because you're starting to become your own person. Your unique, individual personality is taking shape, and the way you relate to others is shifting. Suddenly you don't like the same things you used to—board games and dolls seem a little childish now. You're not really into climbing trees or playing in the creek anymore. Your parents are obviously not used to the new you, so that's going to cause some conflict while they adjust. Same thing with your friends—if they're not changing at the same exact pace and in the same exact way as you, you might grow apart. But that's OK. It's OK to try out new things and new people. The new you has to find its own place in the world. And it's not always easy. When you don't really know who you are yet, it's really difficult to figure out how others see you, and how you want to see yourself.

but who am i?

Sometimes, instead of figuring out your own personality, it seems easier to just adopt that of your friends. But then you're even more unsure of who you really are—like a TV star who's been playing the same role for so long that when the show's over, she's lost. But school makes it really hard not to go along with the pack. Kids can be tactless, aggressive, merciless. Someone who's afraid of being teased about his weight may overcompensate by picking a fight with anyone who looks at him wrong. Another person might hate being called a stick and take her revenge by inventing horrible nicknames for everyone else in the class. Unfortunately, most schools are full of people teasing and excluding one another. The good news is, this kind of atmosphere won't last. It'll ease up a little in high school, and by college it'll be over with completely. Once everyone's a little older and a little more sure of themselves, there's no need to lash out anymore, and people get along a lot better.

am i ugly?

Psychologists recognize adolescence as a time when people are especially focused on themselves—it's called adolescent egocentrism. You think your nose is too big, your thighs too fat, your teeth too crooked, your legs too hairy. And you think that everybody sees exactly what you see. You're obsessing over whether the girls at the pool noticed your love handles, or whether the guys in homeroom are staring at the huge zit on your chin. But the thing about egocentrism is that the stuff it makes you believe—that you're the only one to have such horrible flaws, and that everyone is focusing on you—isn't true. Think about it: if everyone is especially focused on their own problems, then they can't be focusing on yours! The truth is, we all see our flaws as much more obvious than they really are to other people.

the first steps

Don't get us wrong—accepting that your so-called flaws are not actually as bad as you think they are doesn't mean you shouldn't make an effort to look and feel your best. You want to look like yourself—that's how you'll be most attractive—so we're not talking extreme makeovers here. Just try to find a style that you feel comfortable in. It helps if you get to know yourself—what colors you feel most confident in, what kinds of clothes are flattering to your shape (hint: form-fitting clothes are

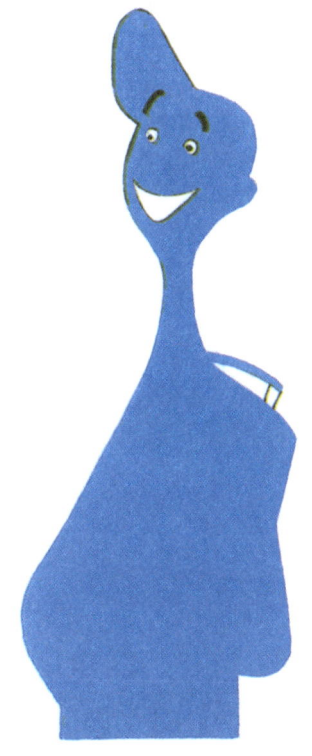

usually more flattering than baggy ones on anyone—seriously!). Be as familiar with your good features as you are with your weaker ones, and try to always show off your best attributes.

Fashion magazines can be great inspiration, but girls (and guys for that matter) should be careful about trying to be just like the people in the photos. Most "real people" are never going to look like Gisele Bündchen or Naomi Campbell. They're professional beauties who work at being glamorous and perfect every day—it's their job, they get paid for it. If your job was to let a twenty-person staff buff and polish you all day long, then you could look glamorous, too! And don't forget about the airbrushing and retouching that happens to every photo before it goes in the magazine—if Naomi has a zit the day of the photo shoot, no problem, it's gone with the click of a mouse. (However, Naomi herself has to keep walking around with the zit.)

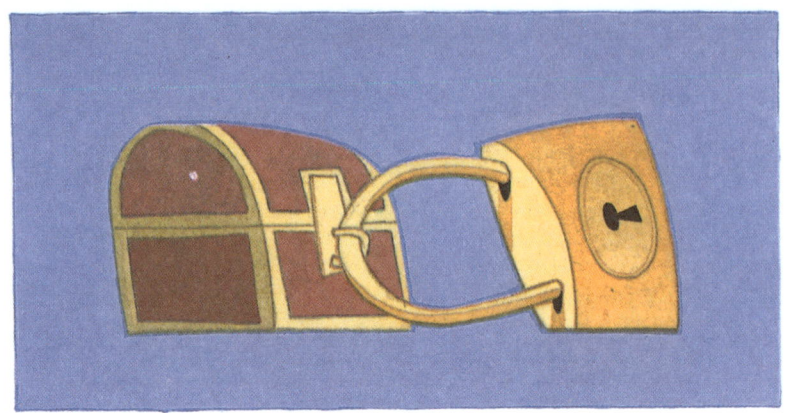

mood swings

You know when everything's going well, you've been laughing and joking with friends, and then you get home and suddenly you're in your bedroom and you feel really down? Everything looks bleak for no reason. Your parents ask what's wrong and that just makes it worse, so you snap back, "Nothing!" And it's actually the truth—you're not sure what's wrong, you just feel bad. You might have heard of mood swings in relation to hormones and PMS (premenstrual syndrome), but both boys and girls have raging hormones, and they can wreak havoc inside anyone.

The good thing about a case of the blues is that it tends to pass within a couple of hours. To speed up the process, try to figure out if there's anything going on that's upsetting you—you might have to dig down deep before you get at the problem. Once you have it, you can take a step toward fixing it—talk to whomever's involved and try to resolve things. But if you've thought about school, friends, home, and everything and you're coming up empty, here's a tip: Get up and do something constructive. It could be anything—kicking a ball around, cleaning your room, taking a shower. Just getting outside of your head for a few minutes can really help break you out of a funk.

let yourself go

Another strategy? Let it all out! Adolescence is a time of excess. If your feelings and emotions are running high, so will all your worries and concerns. Right now the slightest thing can send you over the edge, making everything appear either rosy or black. You can be laughing one minute and crying your eyes out the next. So why not just go with it? Wait till you're at home and then open the floodgates. Alone in your room, a little moaning and wailing can be like therapy—after a few minutes, you get sort of bored with it and you actually start to feel better. Letting yourself cry means you're acknowledging your feelings, telling yourself that you're justified in being upset.

If, on the other hand, you want to break down to your mom or dad or sister, that can be good, too. Being true to your feelings in front of them lets them know you need a little help right now. Tell them what's going on and give them the chance to offer support.

if only i were
more like . . .

Do you know exactly how you would finish this sentence, because you think these exact words all the time? What might be causing your blues is a case of the greens—that is to say, envy. Even if you're levelheaded enough not to obsess over celebrities in magazines, it's harder not to notice the other girls and guys right there in your class and compare yourself to them. Envy can come in different forms, but all will almost certainly bring you down.

The most obvious is looks—if only you had her beautiful straight hair, if only you had his clear skin. Then you'd be happy, right? But just remember the thing about how everyone is more critical of themselves—the kids you wish you were more like probably have about fifteen things they hate about their appearance. But you don't notice those fifteen things. And chances are, someone out there sees you the same way, is wishing they had hair/nails/legs/skin just like yours, and doesn't notice whatever parts you're trying to wish away.

The same goes for other kinds of envy, like wishing you were rich like this kid, or athletic like that kid, or popular like another kid. These kids might in fact be rich, athletic, and popular, but they also all have problems of their own. No one's life is perfect. The best thing to do is compete only with yourself—try to beat your best time on the track, try to look as great as you can look. And when you're feeling down, think about all your strengths and the good things going on in your life that might make others envy you.

mom and dad's
clone

Up until now, whenever you hurt yourself, you would have a good cry, and your mom or dad would arrive on the scene, console you, and make it all better. They were superstars, heroes, able to solve any problem, and you trusted them completely, blindly. When they used to say to you, "There, there, it'll get better soon!" you believed them and suddenly it did get better. But now that you're older, you realize your parents can't solve every problem. They're not superheroes. They have their own problems and concerns—and they don't always hide them from you anymore. Being an adult doesn't make you right all the time. Mom and Dad don't have a monopoly on truth. They are at a stage in life where they've seen things go wrong along the way and they often feel frustrated or regretful. And they might see you as a way of setting things right.

How exactly does that work? A father might urge his son to try out for the soccer team, because he had a great time playing the sport when he was younger and wishes he still could now. Or he might get angry when his daughter brings home a bad report card, because he wants to send her to college—something his family couldn't afford to do for him. (Moms can be guilty of this stuff, too, by the way.) Your parents may harbor a secret (or even subconscious) desire to make you turn out just like them. But you're not obligated to be their clone—you don't have to feel guilty about looking like you want to look and doing the activities you want to do (provided they're safe!). If this is causing conflict in your family, explain to your parents (calmly and rationally) that you're old enough to be treated like your own person, even if it's not exactly the same person they hoped you'd be.

we always hurt the ones
we love

Every family has conflict. Fighting with anyone feels bad, but fighting with people you love can be frightening, devastating, and guilt-provoking. You can't believe the people who are supposed to love and care for you are treating you this way. But you also can't believe you're screaming such awful, cruel things at them, most of which you don't really mean. The thing is, it's because we love people that we care enough to fight with them—who cares if a random person on the street doesn't like the person you're dating? It certainly wouldn't be worth fighting over. But your parents care deeply about you, and they desperately want to protect you. Understanding this can help you see where they're coming from. If a fight with your parents ever gets physical and they hurt you, tell another adult whom you trust as soon as possible (a teacher or guidance counselor are great choices). Otherwise, try not to leave family conflicts unresolved; they'll only get worse. Life at home will be a lot happier if you can get to the root of problems and reach a compromise. (For more help with parents, turn to page 66.)

phase 3

relieve stress through sports

BANISH THE

WRITE IT DOWN

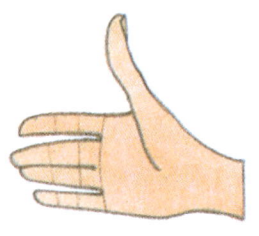

CROSSING THE ROAD WITHOUT FEAR

find a real friend

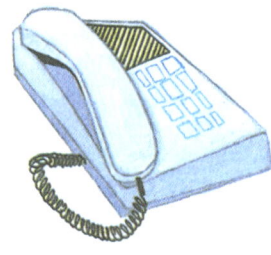

BLUES!

emerge from your cocoon

become an ARTIST

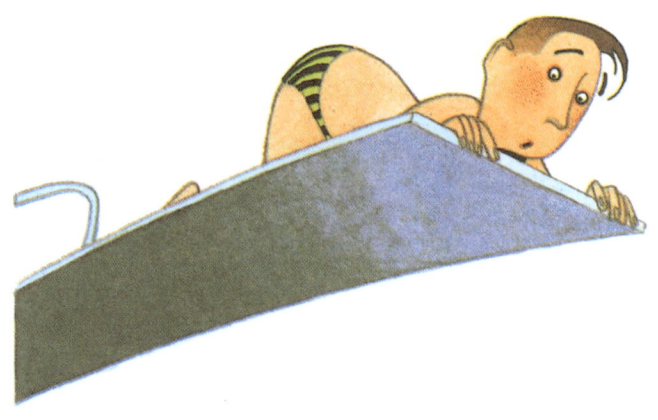

help!

All the low moments, confusion, and frustration that come along during adolescence are very familiar to psychologists. They all agree that they're common phenomena for young people—they're almost inevitable. Most might even say that these problems are so normal that it would be weirder if you didn't encounter them. Not that this makes them any easier to deal with. What you're feeling is very real. You can't just take an aspirin and make it go away. It's something you feel deep inside, something difficult to define.

However, there are things you can do to make getting through this difficult period a little easier. You probably already know that the worst thing you can do when you have a problem is to keep it to yourself.

talk to someone

It's really important to let your feelings out into the open and discuss them with someone. Keeping them bottled up only makes you feel isolated and alone, like you're the only one who's ever gone through something like this. But who do you ask for help when the last people you want to talk to are the ones who ask the most questions (in other words, your parents)? What about older brothers and sisters, if you have them? They're a great choice (especially for commiserating about Mom and Dad!) but depending on your relationship, confiding in them can still be hard. It requires putting yourself out there and hoping they're good enough people not to laugh at you or use the information against you. What you really need is a true friend.

a real friend

The best solution is to confide in a true friend. A friend is someone to whom you can tell anything—your hopes, problems, desires, even your deepest secrets. You can get along well enough with certain friends to joke about teachers, their grading practices, and how they haven't changed their socks for weeks. You can talk to them about the geography teacher who never stops saying the word "consequently" in class. But you never really discuss intimate subjects with them—you don't know how they'd respond; they might sell you out for a laugh. These kinds of friends are just school buddies, acquaintances.

A proper, true friend, one you can be yourself with, is indispensable. We all put on something of an act in public—even people who are really genuine and honest don't go blabbing their innermost secrets all through the halls. But you can tell them to a true friend; you can tell him or her everything and anything, even the things you aren't proud of. The most important point about a real friend is that you can trust him or her.

You can tell him how you hate changing in the locker room because of how you look. You can tell her that it makes you uncomfortable when the gym teacher touches you to help you onto the parallel bars. He/she won't think you're weird or crazy, and won't reveal your secrets to anyone else.

look in the
mirror

At a time when you're questioning so much about yourself and the world, being able to ask someone else what they think really helps. It's great to have a friend who can encourage you when you are not feeling very confident. And a friend can keep you from obsessing about the same thing for hours—the inner monologue turns into a dialogue. Instead of letting you keep on analyzing what some guy's remark meant for hours on end, she'll say, "I think it meant this," and then you can move forward. And more often than not, the conversation will end in fits of laughter instead of more moping. Your friend doesn't have to be someone exactly like you. In fact, you might have one thing in common—maybe you met at drama club practice—but other than that you're entirely different. What matters is that you click, you understand each other, and you care about each other.

If you can manage to find just one friend who fits this description, little things will begin to improve. You'll have someone to sit at the lunch table with—and suddenly the gross mystery meat is more amusing than it is depressing. Walking through the busy, crowded halls together, you won't feel so anonymous.

And when you're really stressed out one day because your grades are so bad your dad is going to explode even though it's not really your fault, you know you can call your friend up and she'll say, "I know! It's totally not your fault! Your dad has to understand if you just explain what happened."

Right about now, you might be thinking, "OK, I get it! Friends are great! But that's the whole problem—I don't have any!" Good point. Not everyone is lucky enough to have found a true friend yet. But don't worry, we've got you covered....

how to make
new friends

Making new friends can be difficult if you've just moved to a new town or started at a new school. Actually, you know what? It's difficult even if you've been in the same place your whole life. It seems like everyone already has their tight-knit little groups and they don't need any new members. But the great thing about friends (unlike, say, boyfriends or girlfriends) is that people are allowed to have more than one. In fact, there's no limit to how many friends people can have, so there's always room for one more. You just have to be brave and make the first move. Start by inviting a guy or girl from your class over to your house—if you've got a school project you could say you want to work on

it together; that'd be an even less stressful way to do it. Whatever you do, don't stay in your shell. If you ever see anyone in the cafeteria or at a football game who looks like they're hanging out alone—in other words, they're in the same boat as you—go up and talk to him or her. You'll both be glad you did.

So what if you're sort of a loner right now because you don't like any of the kids in your class? If this one seems too arrogant, that one too stuck up, this one too fake, and that one too weird, it may be time to ask yourself if you're being a little too picky. Make an effort to understand them before you write them off. Perfect people don't exist, and besides, your first impressions of people could be way off base. Go easy on others. Try to accept them with all their faults, and who knows—you might be able to bring the arrogant one down to earth or help the fake one feel comfortable enough to be herself.

Either that, or you might discover that the guy you thought was weird is actually really funny and his desert-dry sense of humor totally cracks you up. Or that the girl you thought was stuck-up was just shy. Now that you know them all better, you see all sides of them, not just the outside image.

something in common

Another way to find a sympathetic friend is to seek out someone who's going through the same things you are—for example, if the reason you're both so out of it right now is that your parents are getting divorced. Roughly a million children each year are told their parents are divorcing, so (unfortunately) there are plenty of people you know who can relate to your experience. If you go to a small school, you might already know about everyone's family situation, so you can approach someone whose parents have split up, being honest and straightforward: "Hey, can I ask you a question? My parents are separating, and I was just wondering, when it happened to you, how did you deal with having to leave town to go to your dad's house every other weekend?" If you don't know anyone off the top of your head, you can easily work it into conversation when talking with various classmates: "I'm never going to get this Spanish homework done—I have to go to my dad's house all weekend.... Are your parents still together?"

get moving!

Talking to someone isn't the only way to let your feelings out. While opening up is a vital and important one, there are other outlets for your emotions and other ways of coping with anxiety. The first is physical activity. It doesn't matter if you love your body or you hate it—just move it, run it, jump it, give it fresh air, wear it out. Take it out for a spin and see what it can do. When you're down, there's nothing better than a long bike ride, a game of football with some friends, a crazy dance session in the privacy of your bedroom, or swimming so many laps that you're completely waterlogged by the end.... After a little huffing and puffing, the worries just seem to go away.

If you've never participated in any sports or physical activities and aren't sure how to begin, start with a visit to your school's student activities office (if you don't have one, a guidance counselor should be able to tell you what teams and extracurriculars your school offers). A local community center may also be a good source of information—

many towns offer free or inexpensive "adult education" classes in things like dance and aerobics. Towns also frequently have community sports leagues—look up the number of your town hall in the phone book and just ask whoever answers. Organizations like the YMCA can also help with classes, fitness equipment, and use of a swimming pool at a low cost.

so much to choose from

Just because your dad was quarterback of his high school football team, and constantly reminds you of his famous touchdown, don't limit yourself to just one kind of activity—try as many as you like till you find the one or two that you like best. If you feel you have a lot of bottled up aggression, go for a contact sport (like football, wrestling, or hockey), or a high-energy sport (like basketball, soccer, or track), which will allow you to vent it.

If you're not really a team player, try tennis or gymnastics (you're still technically on a team, but competition is individual). If you feel too out of shape to run around a lot, think about swimming, judo, volleyball, dance, skiing, or snowboarding.

If none of these traditional sports appeals to you, "think outside the box" as they say. How about figure-skating? (Most ice rinks offer classes at all levels.) Or rock-climbing? Or surfing? Or spelunking (exploring caves)? There really is something out there for everyone.

If gym class at school is the worst period of the day, don't think that physical activity isn't your thing. So much depends on the teacher: he or she can make you love or hate an activity. There is surely a subject you used to hate but now love because the teacher always has so many good stories and jokes to make the class more fun.

your safety valve

Physical activity allows you to release pent-up energy. The stress involved in growing up really makes it accumulate, but there's no outlet for it just sitting in class all day long. Think of a soda can: if you shake it, everything comes bursting out when you pop the top. But if you take the top off gradually, in a controlled way, it's a lot less messy. Letting off "carbonation" gradually, every day, through physical activity is better than letting it finally burst out in a rage at your teachers, friends, or parents.

If you had to come up with an advertising campaign to promote getting active, you'd never run out of ideas. It makes you look good. It makes your body more flexible, more graceful, more coordinated. If you're overweight, it will help you shed a few pounds. It's healthy. It strengthens your bones and your heart, and it helps you think more

clearly. It releases endorphins—hormones inside your body that bring on feelings of euphoria. Team sports in particular help you to find where you fit into a group. They give you a place where you automatically belong and help you make new friends.

When you join a team or club, you'll also be able to distance yourself from your family and meet other adults—namely, your coach or instructor. Mom and Dad are great, but at an age when you're looking for role models, the more the better. Because physical activity allows you to push yourself to your limits and beyond, it is one of the greatest joys around.

One day, my local community center organized a hike to a nearby mountain. At first, I complained because we had to walk and walk, but after a while, I got into it. I obviously didn't want to get left behind! When we got to the top, after a really strenuous trek, it felt so good. We could see across the hilltops, all the way to the ocean, and we were all shouting like crazy. We were practically high from excitement.

—Patrick, 13

set yourself
free

We could easily bore you with page after page about how great sports are, but there will always be a few who insist that they don't like sports. There are other ways to get up and get out there, to forge new connections in the world. The main thing is to do it, stop sitting around, check out as many places as you can, and mix with a wide range of people of all ages. If the smell of locker rooms and sweatsocks isn't your thing, go to the library, join a drama club, play chess, get involved with a charity or political organization, find a club for computers, stamp collectors, photography, astronomy... There are so many opportunities out there; why not start taking advantage of them?

create
something

Get artsy! Learn a musical instrument, paint a still life, or join a theater group. These activities are all great for overcoming shyness and learning to accept feedback from others. It can be hard at first, to be the one out front whom everyone is looking at or listening to, but it doesn't take long to get used to being the star. And it's great for the ego: suddenly what you do is noticed by others.

Participation in any kind of artistic group is a fantastic way to learn about life. Getting together with a bunch of friends to put on a play will keep you too busy for any self-obsessed worries. You'll be too involved with the adventure and the new challenges. It's also a great way to channel your energy and express what you're feeling inside. This is also true for music, studio art (like painting, drawing, sculpture, ceramics, etc.) and dance (which—bonus!—counts as art *and* physical activity).

I sing in my local choir. I'm the youngest, but the director insists that I come to all the performances because he thinks I have a great voice. It's really scary when we get lined up in a semicircle around the orchestra pit, but when I start singing, I forget all about it. It's like I'm in a different world. And when the audience applauds at the end, I get a huge lump in my throat. I almost feel like crying, but it's not from sadness....

—Maria, 14

Many incredibly shy people have found a way to combat their isolation in the arts, including lots of famous people. The young composer Frédéric Chopin was one such artist, who plunged his heart and soul into music in order to escape loneliness. Why not you?

All artistic activities can be good for you because they offer a way to let out all those emotions you feel inside.

poetic license

When I was a teenager, poetry helped me a lot. I thought I was Emily Dickinson, Oscar Wilde, and William Shakespeare all rolled into one. At night, if I was feeling down, I would scribble my poems in a small, spiral-bound notebook, or I just wrote down everything I was feeling in my diary. I think that the best way to deal with all those deep-seated emotions is to bring them to the surface, and expose them by giving them a form, even if the form is only words on paper.

—Michel, the coauthor

Adolescence is a time for soul-searching: you need to talk about yourself and look at yourself in order to better understand who you are and how you feel. Poetry is one way to do this.

If you're not convinced, read this poem, written by Hillary, a junior-high-school student:

In black ink, I write the pain of injured souls
And the grief of forgotten dreams
I write my lost tears, searching in vain
For the warmth of hands that wipe them away.
I write the black of night, starless,
And the dying glance of fading flowers.

In green ink, I write
The springtime of my life
I write my land, my kingdom, I write my garden
Of youth, and of all the dreams I planted there.

In red ink I write the flames of my ravenous anger.
I write the blood of my lost freedoms
I write the blaze that fuels the fire of my rage.

In blue ink, I write the distant sky of my desires
Of my unrequited dreams.
I write my gaze which is lost in the waves
Of the sea in summer's June.
I write the gentle sky blue of lost loves.

—Hillary, 13

phase 4

ANGER

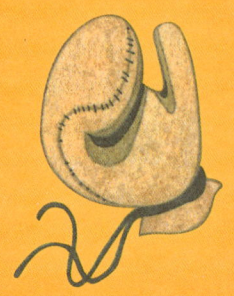

PARENTS

using your judgment in difficult situations

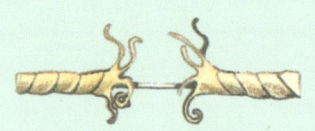

failure at school

brick-wall parents, invisible parents

DOOR SLAMMING, FACE SLAPPING

and

TEACHERS

never think you're not worth it

anger and aggression

Adolescence could be an incredible time, since it offers so many opportunities for fun, excitement, and discovery—if not for the annoying parents, inflexible teachers, mean classmates, and constant change.

It might seem like your parents and teachers are ganging up together to make your life miserable—they can both add to your already heavy burden of worry and self-doubt. And they can really make you frustrated and mad sometimes.

Anger is necessary. It's part of life. Anger at authority figures allows you to break away from childhood and become your own person. (After all, if we never found anything wrong with our parents, we'd never go out and lead our own lives—we'd all live at home forever!) At sixteen, eighteen, or twenty, whenever you become an adult in the eyes of both you and your family, all the conflict and fighting will fade away, and you'll relate to one another in a whole new way.

give me some
space!

"**Put on a sweater,** pick up your dirty socks, tie your shoes, be polite at school, comb your hair, you look like a ragamuffin..."

Even if you're old enough to be in junior high or high school, your parents might still treat you like a baby. And as you get older, it only gets harder and harder to accept their interference with what you wear, who your friends are, even how much salt you put on your food. Their constant nagging—while really just a sign of their concern—is nonetheless suffocating you: "Where are you going? What time will you be home? Will your friend's parents be there?"

Many kids feel like their parents don't trust them, that they don't consider them as separate individuals—more like possessions or pets. If the arguments, disagreements, and standoffs are becoming more and more frequent at your house, remember that your mom and dad are so used to telling you what to do that it's hard for them to see when it's time for a change.

parents just don't
understand

How can they, you're thinking, when it's been eons since they were young? They don't remember the time when their circle of friends was the center of their universe. So when you tell them you need this pair of dark denim jeans with frayed edges, not the crappy, generic, discount-store pair, they don't get that it's because looking good and fitting in is top on your priority list at the moment. Whether it's right or not, what you look like sends out a message about where you belong—with the preps, the Goths, the skaters, or none of the above. So why not remind your parents of that next time they insist you try on something that is completely not you. If money's an issue, try to set up a clothing budget where you're allowed to blow it all on the perfect jeans or buy a bunch of less expensive stuff. (But no complaining that you have nothing to wear after you choose the jeans!) That way, you spend the same amount of money no matter what, but you make your own decisions based on what's important to you.

how the adult mind
works

A word of advice: if you want your parents to trust you, just give them proof that you've grown up. First, be honest—lies are almost always found out eventually, and they make you look really childish and untrustworthy. Second, learn to calmly and rationally negotiate diplomatic solutions: "If you let me go to the party tomorrow night, I promise to have all my homework done beforehand." Third, don't let them wait on you hand and foot—that stuff's for little kids. Show them instead that you're capable of getting your own breakfast in the morning, or organizing your own closet without their help. It doesn't make sense to ask your parents to trust that you're old enough to stay out late or throw your own birthday party if you then turn around and ask them to treat you like a child by returning your library books for you, cleaning up after you, or bringing in your science homework when you forget it. Your parents will always be there to help you out, but the more you act like an adult, the more adult privileges they're likely to give you.

overprotective parents

It's just the way life is: some kids have parents who let them do anything, and some have super-strict parents. You didn't choose them, but you're stuck with them. Does this sound familiar?: Every time you want to go out, it's a battle. They think the world beyond your front door is a jungle populated with bad guys who might, at any minute, rob, rape, con, kidnap, drug, and kill you, if only given the chance. If your parents had it their way, you'd never leave the house or see your friends.

They don't like you going out, and going out is what makes you happiest. So you can only assume they don't want you to be happy. How can you become your own person if you don't participate in the world around you? One girl dealing with overprotective parents wrote about it in this poem:

What's going on, I'm suffocating here
There's nothing in the air to breathe
All I want to do is live
Without always being told what I should or should not do
Do you understand, let me live
You, my parents, you gave me life
That's fine, I'm not complaining
Once, I was your little girl
Though I can hardly remember that time
At all
Please don't forget I've grown
Even if you don't want to understand it
Or accept it . . .
You haven't been left alone, I'm still here, I exist.

—Nicole, 15

You're right to want to go out, to cut the cord, to see what life has to offer. But your parents have legitimate concerns; they're legally responsible for you until the age of eighteen. What they do remember about being young is probably all the dangerous stuff you can get into. They want you to ease into adulthood carefully. After all, if you wanted to teach someone to swim, you wouldn't throw them off the side of a boat and head back for shore, right? You'd have them wade in first, and teach them a few strokes while you stood by.

Obviously we're not in favor of parents who lock their children away from the world (to actualy do this is illegal!). Just realize that your mom and dad aren't crazy or paranoid: going out can be dangerous, especially when it comes to riding in cars with young drivers, being out on the street alone after dark, or trying substances like alcohol or drugs. They just want you to come home in one piece.

slamming doors

Wouldn't it be nice if you could talk things out with your parents? Wouldn't it be nice if you could confide in them? Trouble is, it's hard to find the words, even if you could get them out. Does it ever feel like you've lost the ability to speak when it comes to your parents? That can be a problem, especially when they don't seem to be any better at communicating with you.

"I don't know how it happens," says John, eleven. "As soon as we start talking, it turns into an argument. I can feel it rising up inside me. There's nothing I can do about it, and then I say things that I regret later on. We never agree on anything. Sometimes I'd like to tell them that I do love them, but I just can't. The words don't come out."

Communicating can be a very difficult thing. How can you explain what you mean to someone else, if you're not even sure yourself? Instead of the brilliant arguments in your head, out come temper tantrums, demands, and slammed doors.

Our advice: Go into every discussion with a cool, level head—not rage. Plan what you want to say beforehand, start sentences with "I feel..." instead of "You always..." or "You never...," and try not to whine or raise your voice. With luck, all this will keep both sides from getting into a yelling match.

keeping your
distance

The famous psychologist Dr. Sigmund Freud had a theory that as soon as adolescence hits, boys have a natural desire to move away from their mothers, because they represent the taboo of incest (and, likewise, girls move away from their fathers). Modern psychologists don't all agree with that exactly, but they do agree that it's natural for teenagers to assert their independence. But how do you know exactly how far to distance yourself? And what do you tell the little kid inside you who still wants to be near Mom and Dad?

You're definitely not the only one asking these questions, whether consciously or subconsciously. So many fathers have a hard time accepting that their darling baby daughter is no longer daddy's little girl. Many a mother has wanted to keep holding the hand of her son, who's now at least six inches taller than her. Your growing up announces the beginning of the end for them. Watching you get older means that they themselves are getting older. It means you'll soon be able to fend for yourself, and they fear you won't need them anymore.

a time of
paradox

So when it comes to your parents, you're between a rock and a hard place. You're split between the desire for them to leave you alone, and a secret longing that they'll still look out for you. You're being pulled in two directions: On the one hand, you want independence, on the other, you want security. You'd like to shake free of your parents' grip, but this also makes you a little scared and maybe guilty, too. So if you're experiencing two forces, one pushing forward and the other pushing back, you don't make much progress at all. You're at a standstill. This can make you feel even more frustrated, like you just want to fight with them, sometimes just for the sake of fighting. So many unspoken things are building up that every encounter with them ends in arguments or tears.

So you provoke them. You might not even realize when you're doing it. You'll refuse to clean up your room—even though you are kind of getting sick of walking over the piles of clothes. But you just don't want to do it! Or you'll say the opposite of what your mom or dad says, no matter what that is—they say it's a great day outside, you say, "No, it's not; it's cloudy." They say you look nice today, you say, "No, I don't; I look terrible!" Or you'll wear something you know they'll hate just to annoy them. Even using slang is a way to exclude them and send them the message that you don't even speak the same language anymore.

emerging

Mealtimes often become verbal showdowns when you're a teenager. Adolescence is a time for forming opinions on society and the world around you. Your sense of judgment is becoming more refined. One consequence: you start seeing flaws in your parents' logic and positions on certain issues. So you can't help but argue with them. How can they overlook their own actions (little white lies, compromises, selfishness, rudeness, pettiness) while they condemn these things in

opinions

others—and you?! How can they tolerate world hunger, poverty, racial discrimination, and other injustices that seem so shocking and unacceptable to you? Then there are the parents who smoke, but tell their kids not to. Who use bad language, but tell their kids not to. Who criticize others, but tell their kids that's not nice to do. Things get more and more heated, and then the arguments explode. It can be a volatile, potentially explosive time.

necessary

All this fighting isn't as serious as it might seem. Conflict serves a purpose—it's only through struggle that we find real harmony. By confronting your parents, you're toughening yourself up while still staying connected to them. It's like a boxer in training. He needs a coach to fight with in order to strengthen himself. Those who love you are the perfect people to fill this role, as long as you don't push it too far. If you feel like things are getting out of hand, that you're going to say something you'll regret, it's better to just say, "I need a break, can we talk about this again later?" and go take a walk or go to your room and listen to music for a while. You don't want to permanently injure your coach. Hitting below the belt or taking cheap shots (in other words, saying mean things just to hurt someone) isn't fair play. If ever a fight does get out of hand, don't refuse any attempts at reconciliation. Try not to be stubborn. And instead of returning to the original discussion, which could lead to another argument, talk about something else for a while, or make a joke to defuse the tension. Keeping your sense of humor can soften the blow of a bad fight.

roughness

cut the cord

As we said before, it's best not to argue just for the sake of arguing. Don't say white just because your parents say black. It's a surefire recipe for saying something mean or humiliating—which you will regret the minute the words leave your mouth—and it invites the same thing from your parents. Being disrespectful will always leave you feeling guilty. And that will lead to more worry.

Finally and, most importantly, being argumentative doesn't actually win you more independence or control over your life. Think about it: If you always say and do exactly the opposite of your father, then he still controls what you say and do. To truly become your own person, you need to cut the cord. Disagree when you truly disagree, and agree when you know they're right.

brick walls

Some parents, of course, can remember what it felt like to be a teenager and they understand that your inner turmoil and need for separation is normal. Even if they have a hard time accepting it, they know it's part of the growing-up process. They gradually come to accept the idea that you're no longer a child and that your distance, both physical and emotional, is part and parcel of becoming your own person.

Unfortunately, other parents aren't quite so understanding. They're like brick walls—there's no flexibility, no discussion. Their authority is absolute and they won't tolerate anyone trying to undermine it. Deep down, they might be afraid of becoming useless if they lose the power and privilege of being boss of the family. So they consider your opinions to be ill-informed or naïve or simply not worth listening to because you're not old enough to know better. No matter what you say, their reply is "You're too young to understand." Obviously, they have very poor parenting skills and, short of offering them a parenting manual, there's not much you can do except be patient. They won't be in charge forever. And even if they forbid you from saying certain things, they can't control your thoughts.

The best thing to do, in this case, is to look to other adults in your family or outside of it (aunts and uncles, coaches, your friends' parents…) who can support and guide you.

ghost parents

It might be hard to believe, but there is one kind of parent who's even worse than the brick-wall type: the kind that gives in to everything. We know—it sounds like every kid's dream. But it gets old fast for those who are living it. This kind of parent is happy to let you do whatever you want, which actually has the effect of taking the pleasure out of everything.

By giving in to your every whim, they force you to constantly look for conflict—except it's not really conflict that you want, it's care, concern, and guidance. Even though they can be a pain, rules show you that your parents care, that they aren't willing to just let

you jump out of that boat we mentioned earlier when you've barely learned how to swim.

You want parents who act like parents. This means adults who accept the responsibility of parenting and who know when it's time to say no and assert their authority.

Another kind of ghost parent is the one who's never there, never available because he or she's too busy with work or other commitments. A lot of them think that opening their wallets to buy you whatever you want is enough to compensate. But as much as you love the hundred-dollar sneakers and the leather jacket, they're no substitute for your parents' attention. Love can't be bought. It's OK to point this out to your mom or dad—that you've been missing them lately and want to hang out more often. A conversation would do you all a world of good.

institution

In our society, doing well in school is a sign of achievement (whether or not it necessarily predicts success in real life is up for debate). So your parents can't help but push you to succeed, to work hard and keep getting good grades, so that one day you can get a good job. If your grades slip, of course they're going to be worried. They want you to be safe and secure when you eventually head out on your own, and a decent report card now is the first step in that direction. But that puts a lot of pressure on you not to screw up, which is why discussions about grades often turn into fights.

Since you started junior high or middle school, you've probably heard a lot about how the party's over now and it's time to get serious; you can't breeze through like you might have done in elementary school—all this at a time in life when you have many other (seemingly

alized

more important, less boring) concerns. How can you sit for hours on end in a classroom, then turn around and do homework all night when your mind keeps wandering?

Not easy... especially since school is designed to accommodate the needs of the masses, not the individual. A school is a large, bureaucratic institution. It's not possible for such an institution to take into account the inner workings and personalities of so many students. Some kids grow up faster than others—and at most schools, the teachers have to act in response to the least mature students. That means that at a time when you may be ready and able to intelligently speak your mind and confront and debate the issues, instead you're asked to be quiet, take it all in, and just accept what you're taught. And that can be extremely frustrating.

authority or authoritarians?

You probably also have to deal with some pretty dumb rules, like adhering to a dress code or not chewing gum. Who are these things really hurting, anyway? Apparently some kids tend to stick their gross chewed gum under cafeteria tables or on lockers, and some people are offended or distracted by skimpy tank tops (even though, hello, everybody wears them). So the rules aren't going to change anytime soon, and unless you want detention, you'll just have to deal with them for now, as random and unfair as they seem.

Same goes for your teachers. If you're lucky, you'll have mostly great ones who love their work and know how to help you learn rather than ones who just throw assignments at you. But you won't make it to graduation without at least a couple of "brick-wall" or "ghost" types—the kind who just dispense information and remain distant and inaccessible. Some might even seem like they're personally out to get you. If you really think this is the case—that they're treating you unfairly, grading you more harshly than the other students, or making the entire class's life miserable, speak up. Talk to the teacher first, and if that doesn't work, get your parents and/or the principal involved.

labels

The only way schools have of determining that you're ready to advance to the next grade is with assignments and tests. (Some special schools have decided to banish grades and such, but they're the very rare exception to the rule). It's up to you to adapt to this system of grading. If you do, you'll see that it can actually be satisfying to play along and do well at it, even if you don't buy into the system itself.

Just remember that there's more to you than just your academic reputation. If your French teacher constantly berates you for getting the verbs wrong, it doesn't mean you're doomed to a life of failure. Maybe foreign languages just aren't your strong suit, or maybe her teaching style doesn't mesh well with your learning style. But you certainly have strengths and abilities that this teacher isn't able to see during her fifty-minute class period.

If you can, think of a friend who isn't exactly known for his performance in school. Because you two are close, you know that there are many levels to his personality and that he has plenty of redeeming qualities. Otherwise, you wouldn't be friends.

don't give up

Obviously the school administration judges you by your scholarly aptitude—that's what school is all about. But as long as you're doing your best, try not to take constructive criticism too personally. It's not a judgment of you as an individual. Remember, Einstein's teachers thought he was retarded, and look what he amounted to! Letting yourself slack off because you think "There's no point in trying, I'm just not good at it," isn't going to help anyone.

If you need help, just ask for it. Most teachers are available after class to provide extra assistance, and sometimes that one-on-one attention (without having to worry about asking "dumb questions" in front of your classmates) can make a world of difference. Your school or town might also have a tutoring program—just ask your teacher or guidance counselor. The secret bonus: most teachers are likely to bump up your grades a bit when they know you're making an effort to improve.

Making it through school to graduation is important to your future, whether or not you think you're a great scholar, and whether or not you think you'll ever use what you learned in "real life." Many jobs simply require a high school diploma, and you don't want to be disqualified for those jobs before you even apply by failing out.

However, if school isn't a place that makes you feel good about yourself, find a place that does. Just because you get bad grades in history doesn't mean you can't become a swimming champion, a gifted artist, a great mechanic, a loving friend. Intelligence comes in many forms—emotional intelligence, creative intelligence, even physical intelligence—not all of which are displayed and measured in school.

phase 5

stumbling blocks

TOO MUCH,

getting help

PROFESSIONAL LISTENERS

ANOREXIA AND BULIMIA

RUNNING AWAY AND SUICIDE

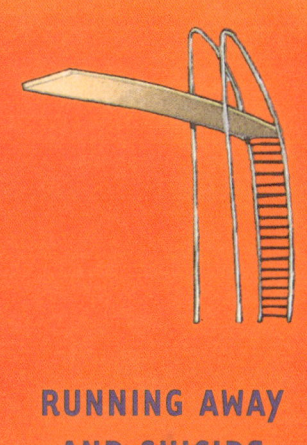

when it's all just too much

it's TOO MUCH

a terrible

Sobbing,
Shrivelling up,
Completely losing hope,
Is that all my life amounts to?

—Brittany, 15

Feeling down now and then is an inevitable part of being human. But after every storm comes a calm. Life will get better again in time.

For most of you, growing up won't be too bad a ride. The changes will happen slowly as the years pass, and you'll come out on the other side relatively unscathed. For those who are self-confident and have

time

some social support from friends and family, the transition to adulthood will seem to happen seamlessly. There might be a few shaky moments, but everything works itself out in the end.

For some others, it's not that easy. "Down in the dumps" becomes such a common feeling that it seems to stifle your whole existence. Or, the arguments at home become so unbearable that all you want to do is run away and never go back. If you feel like your sadness is getting out of control, this section is for you. What do you do when it's all just too much to handle? When you feel like you're being pulled under by a huge, dark wave? When you've hit bottom, with little hope of ever coming back up for air? Know, first off, that there is always hope, and always help available.

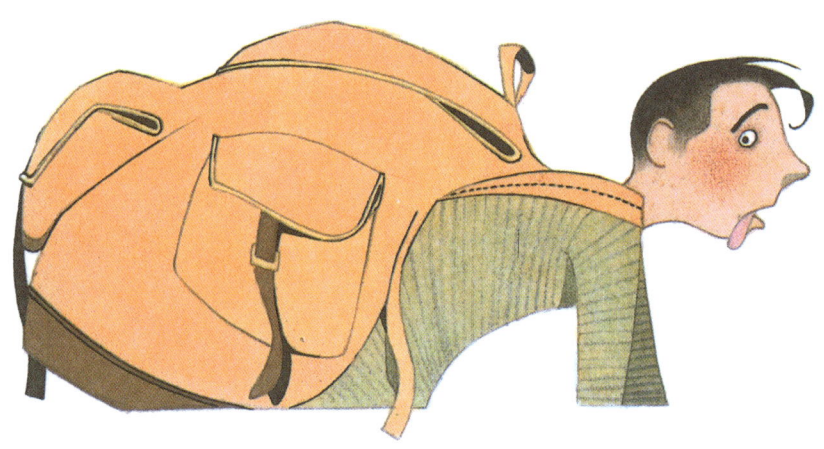

stumbling blocks

If adolescence is smooth sailing for some, why is it such a nightmare for others?

Part of the explanation is that just as we all look different on the outside, our inner workings are also unique. A sad movie can leave some people in the audience indifferent, while it leaves others sobbing their eyes out. Some people are simply more sensitive than others, and some are extremely sensitive. This isn't a defect or an illness (in most cases). On the contrary, it allows for a greater awareness of life. Emotions are felt more strongly, more intensely . . . so intensely sometimes that it can be overwhelming. Where some people may feel washed over by a small wave, you feel swept out to sea. So during adolescence when everyone gets a little more sensitive than usual, you have an especially hard time.

a mountain too high

For others it's not an issue of emotions but of family background. The truth is that life's not fair, and some kids are luckier than others when it comes to parents. You might be stuck with brick-wall types or ghost types, smothering parents, or neglectful parents. Your mom and dad might have problems of their own, like alcoholism or drug use, that affect how they treat you. An unhappy family environment could be directly causing your pain, or it could be the reason you have trouble dealing with other parts of your life—or it could be both.

Abuse doesn't have to be physical to cause damage. But while emotional abuse is harder to define, physical abuse is very clear-cut. If anyone in your family hits you or hurts you—anything more severe than a light slap or spank—you should tell someone as soon as possible. This is also true of a third type of abuse: sexual abuse. No one in your family should be touching you in a sexual way—it's against the law.

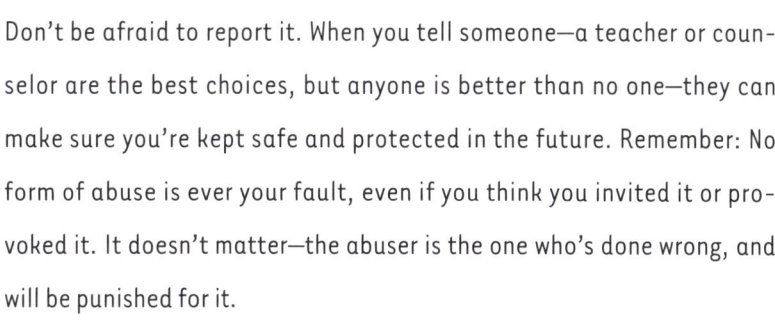

Don't be afraid to report it. When you tell someone—a teacher or counselor are the best choices, but anyone is better than no one—they can make sure you're kept safe and protected in the future. Remember: No form of abuse is ever your fault, even if you think you invited it or provoked it. It doesn't matter—the abuser is the one who's done wrong, and will be punished for it.

what to do?

What do you do when life gets unbearable? What do you do when nothing makes you happy anymore? How do you get back on track?

DEAD END

I'm stuck in a place
Where the boulders are pinning me in
I'm frozen
I can't stand the slightest noise
I want to cry
Something inside is scabbing over
I'm closing up
No one is coming to save me
People laugh at me
People make fun of me
I AM SCREAMING!
But no one is listening
It looks like I have everything
To make me happy
But the important things are missing
Love
Friendship
Confidence
Understanding
As I wait
I withdraw into this shell.

—Laura, 17

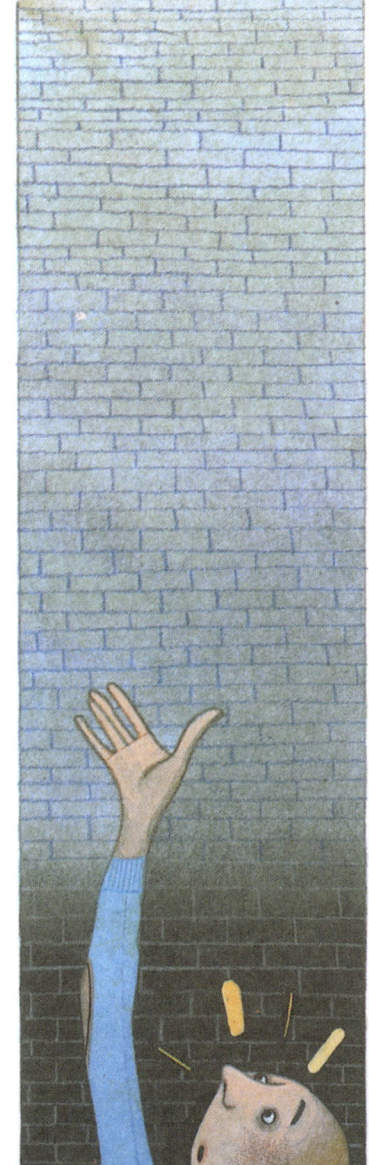

find a way out

This poem, written by a high school student, shows how it feels when you close up inside yourself. A little introspection is a good thing, but your time-out should last just long enough to indulge your feelings and get in touch with your emotions. Stay closed up any longer, and you risk getting used to the solitude, the isolation—and you miss out on life. You don't want to get so caught up in your anxiety that you barricade yourself in your bedroom, avoiding the real world.

Shutting down or cutting off the outside world so you don't have to deal with it only makes things worse. Your parents might not be too much help here—if they like having you tucked in at home all safe and sound more often, they might not encourage you to get back in the game. But you have to. The only way things will ever get better is if you get out there and live.

Most people close off to protect themselves from outside enemies when, in fact, the real enemy is within. It's your own fear. The first step toward overcoming that fear is to stop it from taking over. Never let it make your decisions for you.

Taking action is the best way to shake the blues. If you get involved with some kind of activity—any activity—it will occupy your mind, leaving no room for the dark clouds. In the beginning, you'll probably have to force yourself. Someone will say, "Hey, are you coming to the pool this afternoon?" and you'll think, *No, I don't feel like it.* Don't take no for an answer from yourself! Make yourself go; make yourself participate in any opportunity that comes your way. Slowly but surely, you'll start to want to do stuff, and your favorite activities will seem fun again.

when it's not just
in your head

It's important to listen to the signals your body sends you. If you feel a lot more tired than normal, or are getting a lot of headaches, or any weird new symptom pops up, let your parents know and have them make a doctor's appointment. Sometimes these things can be connected to the way you feel emotionally.

As we said at the beginning of this book, if you're having seriously sad feelings that have lasted for more than two weeks and make you want to sleep all the time or keep you up all night, make you want to eat constantly or not eat at all, and make even joyful occasions seem totally joyless—this can be a sign of true depression. If this sounds like you, a psychologist is the best person to help you work through things. You can get hooked up with one by asking either your guidance counselor or your parents. Don't be afraid that it'll cost too much money—there's probably a psychologist at your school you can talk to for free, or your parents can find one who's covered by their insurance.

There are some other medical things similar to depression that could also affect the way you feel. Intense fear about being around other people—extreme anxiety that you'll say something stupid or embarrassing—is called social anxiety disorder, and it's very treatable. So are panic attacks—occasional bouts of panic that are often accompanied by physical symptoms such as feeling like you can't breathe, like you just have to get out of where you are. Everybody feels these things to some degree at some point, but when they're severe, they're considered serious medical issues. However, doctors have very effective treatments for them.

Two more medical conditions that can develop during adolescence are anorexia and bulimia. These are eating disorders, where people become obsessed with their weight; they think they're fat even though they may be very thin. Anorexics begin to eat less and less food, to the point where malnutrition threatens their health and their lives. Bulimics, on the other hand, binge and purge—that is, they eat a ton of food and then make themselves throw up on purpose, causing, again, malnutrition as well as damage to the digestive system and teeth. Both of these are considered very dangerous medical conditions, so if they sound like you or someone you know, you should tell someone and get help from a doctor immediately.

running away

Whatever the underlying cause, some kids eventually get to a point where they've lost all hope of communicating with their parents, and the only solution to their problems that they can think of is to run away. This affects hundreds of thousands of families every year in the United States.

I'm fed up with my mother who spends her time crying and depressed...
And my father who only knows how to yell.
I'm sixteen; I don't need anyone.
I'm outta here.

—Joe, high-school student

and suicide

The thing is, life is usually just as hard on the street. In order to get money, runaways are often reduced to stealing and sometimes even to prostitution and dealing drugs. Before taking such a drastic step, consider other possible options, like staying with a friend or another relative for a while till things settle down.

Tragically, some kids, even more desperate to get away from a bad situation, attempt to end their lives. Most people at one time or another have thought about the crowd of friends and family crying at their funeral—this is pretty normal. But planning out how you'd do it . . . that's getting into dangerous territory. To actually commit such an act would be the ultimate defeat. Real death is not like actors dying in a movie and then reappearing on screen in another flick three months later. Real death is real. It's forever. It leads to only one place: the bottom of a grave, six feet under.

No matter how hopeless things seem right now, there is ALWAYS hope. If you can no longer face things on your own, there are people to help you, no matter how alone you feel. If you can't tell your parents because they're part of the problem, just tell someone, anyone. (If a friend ever tells you he or she thinks about suicide, or "ending it all," you must tell an adult immediately.) With professional help, things will get better. See page 105 for places to get help.

open arms

There are plenty of people whose whole full-time job it is to help you. Listening and offering advice is what they're there for, and you might be surprised at how many kids actually go see them—guidance counselors, nurses, even teachers you connect with. There are times when you need more than a friend or parent. Psychologists are the people most qualified to help resolve serious inner conflicts. They have the time (more than a regular doctor) and the training to help people work through difficult situations. They can even help to act as a go-between for you and your parents. Trust us: no matter how impossibly tangled your situation seems to you, it'll seem entirely familiar to a psychologist.

the sun'll come out . . .

There are likely many adults in your life who appear to be happy and confident, but have been through some troubled times. They, too, felt unsure of themselves, felt like there was no way out. Maybe they even had dark thoughts about running away or suicide, but they managed to pull themselves out of it and recover.

Beating the blues was probably just the first of many battles they had to overcome through the years, but it made them realize that they had abilities they didn't know they possessed before. The bumpy ride through adolescence prepared them for the unexpected events they would face as adults. Just like them, in a few years you might even look back on these years with nostalgia—thinking how wonderful a time it was when everything was exciting and new and life was full of possibilities.

This age
When there is as much black in your eyes
As there is blue
As much sadness as happiness
As much despair
As there is hope.

—Virginia, 15

Useful Information

1-800-SUICIDE (784-2433)
National suicide hotline open 24 hours a day, 7 days a week that connects you to a counselor at a crisis center near you.

1800-4-A-CHILD (422-4453)
Childhelp USA hotline open 24 hours a day, 7 days a week for kids who are being abused or people who are worried that someone else is being abused.

1-800-656-HOPE
National Sexual Assault Hotline operated 24 hours a day, 7 days a week by RAINN, the Rape, Abuse and Incest National Network.

1-800-999-9999
The Covenant House Nineline, open 24 hours a day, 7 days a week, provides help to homeless or runaway kids, including transportation home or to a safe shelter. You can call to talk about other problems as well-you don't have to be a runaway.

1866-4-U-TREVOR
The Trevor Project 24-hour hotline provides anonymous help to gay and questioning teens.

1-858-481-1515, www.edreferral.com
National Eating Disorder Referral and Information Center provides information and assistance finding treatment for eating disorders like anorexia and bulimia.

www.teenhelp.org
For teens, by teens, this website provides peer support and advice about a variety of issues.

www.nmha.org
The National Mental Health Association can help you find a counselor or psychologist in your area. From the home page, click on the link for Local Support Groups and Treatment Resources.

bibliography

Books

Dolto, Françoise, *Paroles pour adolescents, ou le complexe du homard* (Advice for Teens), Éditions Hatier, 1989

Spitz, Christian, *Questions d'adolescents* (Teen Issues), Le Seuil, 1995.

Poèmes d'adolescents (Teen Poems), Pédagogie Freinet, Éditions Casterman, 1974

Poslaniec, C. (ed), *Adolescences en poésie* (Teen In Poetry), Éditions Gallimard, 1982.

Je voudrais crier (I Want to Scream) (*texts de lycéens*), Éditions Syros, 1992.

Picquemal, Michel, *Paroles d'espoir* (Words of Hope), Éditions Albin Michel, 1995.

Web articles

The National Marriage Project, Rutgers University, 2003.
www.marriage.Rutgers.edu/publications/soou/textsoou2003.htm

Doorery, Marie. "Elkind, David (1931-)," Gale Encyclopedia of Psychology, 2001
www.findarticles.com/cf_dls/g2699/oo4/2699000453/print.jhtml

Web sites

U.S. Department of Health and Human Services, Administration for Children & Families
www.acf.dhhs.gov/programs

index

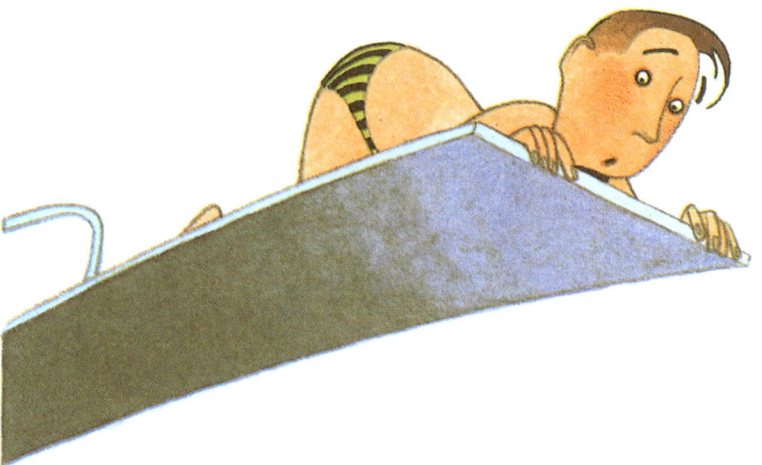

A

abuse, 43, 95
acceptance of others, 51
acknowledging feelings, 39, 47
acquaintances vs. friends, 48
activity for blues, 38, 53–60, 97
adolescent blues, 26–43
   acknowledging feelings, 39, 47
   activity for, 38, 53–60, 97
   anxiety, 9, 33
   attractiveness, 35–37, 40
   boys and sex, 29, 31–32
   celebrities and, 19, 37
   competing with yourself (only), 40
   crying, 39
   egocentrism, 35
   envy, 40
   feelings, acknowledging, 39, 47
   fighting, 33, 43, 66, 73, 78
   flaws, focusing on, 35–37, 40
   friendship shake-ups, 33
   girls and sex, 29, 30, 32
   identity and, 25, 33–34
   insecurities, 22, 34
   mood swings, 38–39
   personality development, 25, 33–34
   questions about sex, 30, 32
   sex, 17–19, 29–32
   style, finding your, 36–37
   teasing, 34
   transformation, 12, 16–17, 28, 29–32
   wet dreams, 31–32
   See also blues, banishing; childhood, farewell to; depression; parents and teachers
adult privileges, 69
alcohol, 23
anger, 33, 43, 66, 73, 78
anorexia, 99
anxiety, 9, 33
artistic activities, 59–60
attractiveness, 35–37, 40

B

blues, banishing, 44–63
   acceptance of others, 51
   acknowledging feelings, 39, 47
   acquaintances vs. friends, 48
   activity for, 38, 53–60, 97
   artistic activities, 59–60
   common, finding something in, 52
   creative activities, 59–60
   divorce, 52
   endorphins from activity, 57
   feelings, acknowledging, 39, 47
   friendships, 33, 47–52
   loners, 51
   making friends, 50–52
   negative self-talk, 49
   "perfect" people, nonexistence, 51
   poetry, 61–63
   self-talk, negative, 49

team sports, 57
"thinking outside the box," 55
See also adolescent blues; childhood, farewell to; depression; parents and teachers
boys and sex, 29, 31–32
"brick walls," 81, 86
bulimia, 99
busy parents, 83

C

celebrities and adolescence, 19, 37
cheap shots, avoiding, 78
childhood, farewell to, 10–25
    alcohol and, 23
    cigarettes and, 23
    decision-making, 15
    drugs and, 23
    in-between period, 23–24
    independence, 15, 24, 25, 69, 74–76
    insecurities, 22, 34
    isolation, feelings, 22–23, 96–97
    personality development, 25, 33–34
    risks in life, 20–21
    rites of passage, 23–24
    role models, 19, 57
    school and, 14–16, 23
    sex, 17–19, 29–32
    transformation, 12, 16–17, 28, 29–32
    world affairs and, 20–21
    See also adolescent blues; blues, banishing; depression; parents and teachers
cigarettes, 23
clones of parents, 41–42
clothing issues, 68
common, finding something in, 52
communication with adults, 73
competing with yourself (only), 40
confronting parents, 78
creative activities, 59–60
crying, 39

D

decision-making, 15
depression, 90–104
    abuse, 43, 95
    activity for, 38, 53–60, 97
    anorexia, 99
    bulimia, 99
    defined, 9, 98
    eating disorders, 99
    emotional abuse, 95
    emotions, differences in, 94

family background impact on, 95
help for, 98–99, 101, 102
hope for, 103–104
isolation, feelings, 22–23, 96–97
learning from, 103–104
panic attacks vs., 99
physical abuse, 43, 95
psychologist for, 98–99, 102
running away, 100–101
sensitivity, differences in, 94
sexual abuse, 95
shutting down, 96–97
social anxiety disorder vs., 99
suicide, 101
symptoms of, 9, 92–93, 98–99
  See also adolescent blues; blues, banishing; childhood, farewell to; parents and teachers
disrespectful, being, 80
divorce, 52
drugs, 23

E
eating disorders, 99
egocentrism, 35
emerging opinions, 76–77
emotional abuse, 95
emotions, differences in, 94
endorphins from activity, 57

envy, 40

F
family background impact on depression, 95
feelings, acknowledging, 39, 47
fighting, 33, 43, 66, 73, 78
flaws, focusing on, 35–37, 40
friendships, 33, 47–52

G
"ghosts," 82–83, 86
girls and sex, 29, 30, 32
giving up, avoiding, 88–89
going out issues, 70–72

H
harmony from conflict, 78
help for
  depression, 98–99, 101, 102
  school, 88–89
honesty, importance of, 69
hope for depression, 103–104

I
identity and adolescence, 25, 33–34
in-between period, 23–24
independence, 15, 24, 25, 69, 74–76
insecurities, 22, 34
intelligence, forms of, 89
isolation, feelings, 22–23, 96–97

L
labeling by schools, 87
learning from depression, 103–104
loners, 51
M
making friends, 50–52
mealtimes, 76–77
money vs. parents, 83
mood swings, 38–39
N
nagging, 67
negative self-talk, 49
neglectful parents, 83
negotiation skills, 69
O
opinions, emerging, 76–77
overprotective parents, 70–72
P
panic attacks vs. depression, 99
parents and teachers, 64–89
    adult privileges, 69
    anger, 33, 43, 66, 73, 78
    "brick walls," 81, 86
    busy parents, 83
    cheap shots, avoiding, 78
    clones of parents, 41–42
    clothing issues, 68
    communication with, 73
    confronting parents, 78
    disrespectful, being, 80
    divorce, 52
    emerging opinions, 76–77
    fighting with, 33, 43, 66, 73, 78
    "ghosts," 82–83, 86
    giving up, avoiding, 88–89
    going out issues, 70–72
    harmony from conflict, 78
    help at school, 88–89
    honesty, importance of, 69
    independence, 15, 24, 25, 69, 74–76
    intelligence, forms of, 89
    labeling by schools, 87
    mealtimes, 76–77
    money vs. parents, 83
    nagging, 67
    neglectful parents, 83
    negotiation skills, 69
    opinions, emerging, 76–77
    overprotective parents, 70–72
    reconciliation, 43, 78
    rules and showing concern, 82–83
    rules of school, 86
    school importance, 84–85
    security vs. independence, 74–76
    sexual education and, 30
    smothering parents, 70–72
    space from, getting, 67, 69
    trust issues, 67, 69
    tutoring programs, 89
    understanding from, 68
    unfair treatment by teachers, 86
    "yes" to every whim, 81–82
    See also adolescent blues; blues, banishing; childhood, farewell to; depression
"perfect" people, nonexistence, 51
personality development, 25, 33–34
physical abuse, 43, 95
physical activity, 38, 53–58, 97
physical transformation, 12, 16–17, 28, 29–32
poetry, 61–63
psychologists, 98–99, 102
Q
questions about sex, 30, 32
R
reconciliation, 43, 78
risks in life, 20–21

role models, 19, 57
rules and showing concern, 82–83
rules of school, 86
running away, 100–101

S

sadness, 9.
    See also adolescent blues; blues, banishing; childhood, farewell to; depression; parents and teachers
school
    childhood, farewell to, 14–16, 23
    help with, 88–89
    importance of, 84–85
    labeling by, 87
    rules of, 86
    See also parents and teachers
security vs. independence, 74–76
self-talk, negative, 49
sensitivity, differences in, 94
sex, 17–19, 29–32
sexual abuse, 95
shutting down, 96–97

smothering parents, 70–72
social anxiety disorder, 99
space from parents, getting, 67, 69
style, finding your, 36–37
suicide, 101
symptoms of depression, 9, 92–93, 98–99

T

teachers. See parents and teachers; school
team sports, 57
teasing, 34
"thinking outside the box," 55
transformation, 12, 16–17, 28, 29–32
trust issues, 67, 69
tutoring programs, 89

U

understanding from adults, 68
unfair treatment by teachers, 86

W

wet dreams, 31–32
world affairs, 20–21

Y

"yes" to every whim, parents saying, 81–82

about the authors

Michel Piquemal is a former teacher who now writes and publishes for young people full time. This is his second book for preteens and teens about depression.

Melissa Daly is a former senior staff writer at *Seventeen* magazine, where she wrote articles and columns on health, sexuality, relationships, and other topics of interest to teenagers. She is currently an editor at *Fitness* magazine. She is a graduate of the College of William & Mary, and she lives in New York City.